Original title:
A Brooch on the Heart

Copyright © 2025 Creative Arts Management OÜ
All rights reserved.

Author: Samuel Kensington
ISBN HARDBACK: 978-1-80586-127-0
ISBN PAPERBACK: 978-1-80586-599-5

The Heart's Jewelry Box

In the chest where feelings dwell,
A sparkly trinket rings a bell.
With laughter shining, bright and bold,
Each silly story never gets old.

A mismatch here, a clasp gone awry,
Jewels that wink like a twinkling sky.
Tickling hearts in a playful dance,
Crafting memories with each fancy chance.

Echoes of the Adorned

Glimmers jingle, echoing cheer,
Whispers of love we hold so dear.
A pendant swings, a tale unfolds,
With giggles wrapped in silver and gold.

Each charm winks with a teasing grin,
Poking fun at where we've been.
Tutorials on fashion from friends so sweet,
We strut through life on mismatched feet.

Connecting Points

In a world strung up like beads on a line,
We laugh at knots that fate designed.
Each twist and turn a quirky jest,
Our hearts link up, forever blessed.

From wrist to wrist, the stories spread,
A ribbon here, some pearly thread.
Dancing between giggles and sighs,
We map our joy beneath the skies.

The Closure of Affection

A clasp that clicks, a funny sound,
Hearts connect, both lost and found.
With every fastened love we share,
We stitch together laughter in the air.

Every layer hides a scheme or two,
A patterned love, quirky and true.
So let us wear these silly things,
And laugh as brightly as jewelry sings.

Frayed Edges of Affection

In the closet, a stashed delight,
A pin that's lost its shiny bite.
It once was bold, now just a tease,
Whispering laughs with quirky ease.

Patterns frayed and colors wild,
Adorning hearts, a playful child.
With each clink, a giggling spree,
Who knew love could be so free?

A Silhouette of Memory

In the shadows, stories play,
Of memories tucked far away.
A vintage clip with tales to share,
Faded laughter hangs in the air.

Hats askew, the dance must go,
Each twist and turn, a thrilling show.
When clipped on joy, how well we spark,
A silhouette, though times are dark.

The Metal of Emotion

Rusty sentiments, polished glee,
Like treasures found beneath a tree.
Each twinkle tells a jolly jest,
With every gleam, my heart feels blessed.

Grinning pins on jackets bright,
Mocking woes with sheer delight.
Metals laugh, they tease and play,
Turning gloom to a sunny day.

Bows, Pins, and Heartbeats

Bows tangled up in careless cheer,
They sway and curl, drawing near.
Pins most likely from times of old,
Winking secrets, stories told.

Heartbeats measure every laugh,
A stitch in time, our finest craft.
With each glance, a giggle sigh,
As bows and pins give life a try.

Glimmers of Affection

In a pocket, there it sits,
A sparkly glitch that never quits.
With every step and little jolt,
My shirt now sports a jewel revolt.

It winks at strangers, catches their eye,
I'm just a walking disco pie!
With laughter trailing where I go,
It's a riot of bling, and all for show.

Adorning the Soul's Embrace

Tucked beneath my deep red coat,
A shiny gem that seems to float.
It's stuck on tight but likes to sway,
Who knew it had a mind to play?

Each wink it gives gives me a laugh,
A comedy act—a shining gaffe.
I swear it plots to steal the scene,
That rascal gem, oh so obscene!

Treasures of the Tender Heart

Nestled near my heart's warm glow,
A quirky gem that steals the show.
It giggles gently when I sneeze,
A raucous notion with such ease.

With each embrace it makes me grin,
A playful jester kept within.
It tosses sparkles, bright and bold,
My secret treasure, a sight to behold!

Embellishments of Emotion

Oh dear, what pleasantries I wear,
A glittering rhyme that's full of flair.
It jumps around like it's alive,
Causing chaos, oh how we thrive!

As I strut down this cheery street,
It's every bit the grand elite.
Who knew a trinket could produce,
Such joy and laughter, let it loose!

A Touch of Elegance

In the attic, a gem so bright,
Found it hiding, what a sight!
Worn with flair, a little tease,
My friends say, 'What a breeze!'

Sparkling pin with a cheeky grin,
It holds my scarf when the winds begin.
Fashion faux pas? Not on my watch,
Though it sticks me, I never botch!

Tokens of Tenderness

A tiny pen, shaped like a cat,
Sticks to my coat, imagine that!
Friends laugh hard, what a display,
'You're a charmer in a quirky way!'

Each little clip has its own tale,
From crafty hands, they set their sail.
I wear them with gusto, oh what fun,
A circus of joy, and I'm the star of the run!

Radiance of the Heart

A glimmer here, a giggle there,
Wearing this pin, I dance in the air.
It sparkles bright like a wink from the sun,
'Watch out world, I'm here, let's run!'

With every dash, it jigs and it jives,
'Bring it on,' it's got a hundred lives.
My fashionista friends just shake their heads,
'You've stitched chaos, love, into threads!'

Dappled Attire

A patchwork badge, looking so sweet,
It matches my socks, oh, what a feat!
With each new look, a smile ensues,
'Where'd you get that?' It's my muse!

Buttons and pins, a glorious array,
They dance on my coat, come what may.
I strut and I preen, in colors so loud,
This patchwork heart, I wear it proud!

The Locket of Longing

In a locket swung with glee,
A tiny heart beats just for me.
It holds my wishes, neat and tight,
Like snacks I stash for late-night bites.

Oh my treasure, gleaming bright,
You sparkle more than morning light.
With every hug and cheeky grin,
You're the magical kin within!

Tokens of Temporal Love

A candy wrapper, crumpled small,
A memory from our first fastball.
Your smile was sweet, your aim was poor,
But oh how that day made me adore!

With coffee stains and scribbled notes,
Our love's a ship without the coats.
Drifting through time, we make it great,
Just like that cookie on my plate!

Shimmering Thoughts

Thoughts like glitter, they drift and float,
Clinging to dreams in my old coat.
With every laugh you launch my way,
I fear I'll burst and float away!

Each whimsy spark, a little jest,
Tickles my heart, oh what a fest!
Like mismatched socks on laundry day,
Our love's a dance in a silly spray!

Affection Worn Close

A button lost, but found with flair,
Stitched on tight, a wacky pair.
Twirling round in mismatched shoes,
We strut our stuff, with nothing to lose!

Worn so close, each laugh we share,
A quirky tale beyond compare.
Like silly hats or wobbly chairs,
This bond we wear is quite the dare!

Heartfelt Enticements

A little trinket shines so bright,
It whispers secrets, day and night.
With every giggle, every tease,
It sways my heart like a gentle breeze.

I wore it once, oh what a sight,
It danced around, oh such delight!
My friends just laughed, they had their say,
'That charm's a rascal, on its way!'

Encircled in Love

With every twist, it spins around,
A circle of giggles, pure joy found.
It pins my heart to silly ways,
Making ordinary, the brightest days.

This charm of jest, it winks with glee,
A friendly poke, come laugh with me!
In tight embraces, it's snug and tight,
Who knew that joy could feel so right?

Charms of Cherishment

Upon my chest, a little spark,
It tickles gently, leaving its mark.
A tiny jest, this charm I wear,
It leaves me chuckling, without a care.

With every jingle, it seems to say,
'Let's find some fun, come what may!'
In friendship's grasp, we twirl and spin,
With laughter's grace, let the joy begin!

Heartfelt Brocade

Threads of laughter, brightly sewn,
A tapestry of joy I've grown.
This playful gem, so full of cheer,
It brightens days, it draws us near.

Wrapped in giggles, soft and light,
It holds our dreams, so warm, so bright.
With every hug, it takes its part,
In stitching smiles upon the heart.

Heartfelt Attachments

With charm that clings like sticky tape,
It laughs and sparkles, can't escape.
A winking pin that steals the show,
What tales it tells, oh, don't you know?

It dances on a lumpy chest,
And never fails to be the best.
If fashion needs a little sprout,
This little gem will pull it out.

A bumblebee on Sunday best,
Or something gold with silly zest.
A treasure tucked in fabric fine,
It whispers quirks, 'This look's divine!'

So if you spot a quirky flair,
It's likely pinned with lots of care.
To all who see it, laughter flows,
A hearty chuckle as it glows.

Threading through Time

In days of old, they wore such art,
With shiny bits to warm the heart.
A trinket here, a doodad there,
A laughing face beyond compare.

From ancient pins to jeweled schemes,
They hang like joy upon our dreams.
Each twist and turn, a giggle grows,
Unraveling tales of highs and lows.

Oh, how they jingle, clink and charm,
Entwining laughter with their warm.
In blinged-out glory, they parade,
A time machine of polka dots made!

So join the fun, don't hesitate,
For every pin can celebrate.
A journey through the worlds we weave,
With every sparkle, we'll believe.

A Symphony of Metal

When shiny metal starts to shine,
It hums a tune that's simply fine.
A clash of colors, oh what glee,
It turns a frown to pure esprit!

Each little piece a bard in tow,
With stories only pins would know.
A maraschino cherry smile,
With every glance, it's worth your while!

The notes they play, a merry dance,
In every glance, a cheeky chance.
To wear the whims of joy in gold,
An orchestra of laughs unfolds.

So fasten tight, let laughter ring,
As every pin becomes a fling.
A concert bright upon your chest,
Where humor finds its lovely nest.

Tokens on a Silken String

A silken thread with treasures bold,
Each little token glimmers gold.
A wink, a nudge, a cheeky grin,
What fun and mischief's locked within!

From safety pins to fancy flair,
Adorning garments with sweet care.
With every twist, a humorous tale,
Of mishaps, laughter, and a sail!

Oh, in a world that likes to stress,
These tokens bring a light finesse.
With every jingle, smiles arise,
Each charm a sprinkle in disguise.

So gather 'round, with laughter bring,
The silly joys that life can swing.
For every pin, a burst of cheer,
A silken string to hold them near!

Jewel of the Soul

In a pocket of dreams, it twinkles bright,
A shiny little gem that feels just right.
It promises laughter, a wink, a snort,
Dancing on wishes like a humorous court.

With each twist and turn, it sparkles with glee,
Telling silly tales of you and me.
It jests like a jester, and never feels worn,
A jewel of the soul, forever reborn.

Ornament of Longing

A bauble of charm, it dangles and swings,
Wishing for laughter, it softly sings.
With a wink and a nod, it tickles your fancy,
This ornament's humor is wild and chancy.

It pulses with joy, a playful delight,
Whispering secrets under moonlight.
Each sparkle, a chuckle, through hopes it does cling,
Creating a melody, making hearts sing.

Pinning the Past

On the fabric of time, it playfully lies,
With giggles of memories and sparkly ties.
A whisper of yesterdays, funny and dear,
   Pinning the past like a pun in the rear.

It jabs at the moments we can't quite forget,
   With pokes and prods, it ignites a duet.
Mirthfully clinging, it shores up the dock,
Building a bridge with each tickle and mock.

A Heart's Keepsake

An heirloom of chuckles, it sits in plain view,
Crafted with smiles, oh so shiny and new.
Comedic and clever, it warms up the room,
A heart's keepsake wearing laughter's costume.

It catches the light with a playful caress,
Turning old frowns into joyful confess.
Each giggle a gem, each snort a delight,
A treasure forever, shining so bright.

Glittering Recollections

In the attic, I found a pin,
Adorned with gems that sparkled thin.
I tried to wear it for a day,
But it slid right off, oh what a ballet!

A fleck of glitter stuck in my hair,
My friends all laughed, 'Do you really care?'
I claimed it's vintage, oh such a catch,
While secretly wishing it had a patch!

Stuck in a dress from ages past,
This shiny relic's quite a contrast.
It wanted to shine, but I had to flee,
Pinned on my blouse, it whispered to me!

Yet when I wear it, I feel so bold,
Like I'm a queen in a story told.
Now every laugh is a joyful art,
With a vintage gem that won't depart!

A Whispered Keepsake

Once I found a gem so bright,
It twinkled 'hello' with all its might.
I donned it proudly for a date,
But it snagged my collar—oh, what fate!

My date was charming, a real delight,
But the brooch was a hooligan, ready to fight.
It launched itself onto his tie,
I laughed so hard, I nearly cried!

He said, 'What's this, a bold new trend?'
I replied, 'Just a keepsake that can't pretend!'
It danced around like it owned the room,
While we sat entranced in its shiny plume.

So now we joke about that night,
The brooch of chaos, pure delight.
A memory pinned with laughter's thread,
Who knew a keepsake could lead to red?

Ties that Bind

A twist, a knot, a silly bow,
We tie our hearts in ways we show.
With laughter wrapped in colored threads,
The fabric of our joy spreads.

In clumsy dances, we collide,
A friendship bond, our trusty guide.
With every snag, a chuckle's near,
We patch it up with kites and cheer.

In funny hats we strut about,
With mismatched socks, we laugh and shout.
Through tangled tales of daily grind,
We wear our scars, the ties that bind.

So let us tease, and poke with glee,
In this odd tapestry, just you and me.
Every stumble, a chance to play,
Together is where we'll always stay.

Charmed Embrace

In quirky hugs and awkward grins,
Here's where our true adventure begins.
With charms of laughter on display,
We wear our quirks throughout the day.

A wink, a nudge, a silly dance,
Each silly move, we take our chance.
With friendship's sparkle shining bright,
We twirl through life, what a delight!

Like mismatched socks, we skip and prance,
In every step, a comical chance.
With charm bracelets jingling loud,
We celebrate as one proud crowd.

So let's embrace the goofball antics,
Life's silly moments, oh so frantic.
In every hug, our spirits race,
We share together this charmed embrace.

Heartstrings and Trinkets

With heartstrings strummed like zany beats,
We dance through life in funny feats.
A trinket here, a giggle there,
In clinking laughs, we find our flair.

A ribbon tied with careless care,
In friendships made, we're light as air.
With every joke and playful tease,
We hang our joys upon the breeze.

Odd little things, our treasure chest,
In silly moments, we feel the best.
With heartstrings tugged, we pull and play,
In this odd dance, we find our way.

So let's collect our trinkets bold,
In laughter's light, our stories told.
In every giggle, a memory sparks,
We wear our joy like shining marks.

The Art of Attachment

With paper clips and silly glue,
We craft connections, just me and you.
In quirky ways, we share our art,
A masterpiece of the mind and heart.

With silly strings and things unplanned,
We navigate this wondrous land.
A giggle here, a poke to tease,
In lovely chaos, life's a breeze.

We sketch our dreams on napkins bright,
In evening chats that last till night.
With every line, a funny flare,
We paint our tales with love and care.

So let us share this wild creation,
With laughter as our true foundation.
In every memory, we'll entrench,
The vibrant joy of our sweet wrench.

Enamelled Feelings

My heart's a canvas, bright and loud,
With colors that show, I'm pretty proud.
Oh, blue for the blues that I sometimes wear,
And red for the laughs that fill the air.

It's shiny with dreams, a playful gleam,
With glittery thoughts that burst at the seam.
Riding a wave of whimsy and cheer,
My heart is a gallery, come visit here!

A Locket of Longing

In a locket, I hide all my whims and my dreams,
A treasure trove bursting at the seams.
Inside it, a snack—well, who doesn't love cake?
A secret recipe—let's see who'll partake!

Every glance at my trinket brings silly delight,
Like a dance with a squirrel in the soft moonlight.
It jingles and jangles, a playful affair,
Each sigh is a giggle that floats in the air.

The Emblem of Connection

A badge of laughter, worn with such pride,
It binds us together like a joyful ride.
With winks and with nods, we share our best jokes,
Our hearts are the magnets, connecting the folks.

It's sewn with the threads of fun and of glee,
A patchwork of moments, just you and me.
Each time that we giggle, it shines ever bright,
An emblem of friendship, a true delight.

Ribbons and Heartstrings

Tied with a ribbon, my heart's in a twist,
A knot full of giggles, should not be missed.
With fluttering bows that dance in the breeze,
Each tug on my heart brings forth silly tease.

Woven together, our quirks sing in tune,
Like cats chasing yarn beneath the full moon.
Our quirks are the threads that keep us in sync,
In this wild, funny world, we laugh, we just think.

Strung Along the Heart

You wore that pin, oh what a sight,
It sparkled like stars on a warm night.
But alas, it fell, with a clink and a clatter,
The dog thought it was food, oh, what a matter!

Chasing the pup, I lost my grace,
Tripping and dodging, what a wild race!
That shiny piece, not made for the chase,
Now it's the prize at the dog's favorite place.

Threads of Sentiment

Stitching emotions with colors so bright,
But my thread got tangled, what a real fright!
Each little knot, like a comic relief,
Made me laugh out loud, amid the grief.

I tried to add sparkle, but it turned to goo,
The fabric now looks like a messy stew.
Yet in the chaos, fun found its way,
A joyful creation, come what may.

A Sparkle in the Shadow

In the corner shone something so bold,
A treasure hidden, a story untold.
But wait, what's this? An old sock nearby,
My fashion sense questioned, oh me oh my!

It glimmered and giggled, my heart took a spin,
How could such odd mates ever fit in?
Laughter echoed through the room's dim light,
A spark in the shadow, what a strange sight!

The Pin that Holds

It started as elegance, a little surprise,
But my cat thought it was a toy in disguise.
Chasing and pouncing, it flew through the air,
The pin now a projectile, nothing could compare!

It landed on Grandma while she sipped her tea,
She blinked in confusion, 'Oh dear, is that me?'
With giggles erupting, we shared a good laugh,
That incidental comedy stole our evening's half.

Embellished Emotions

In a world full of sparkles,
Each pin's got a story to tell,
Like the time I lost my lunch,
A brooch caught it quite well.

Glittery hearts on my sweater,
Pinch my fabric, and I squeal,
Every time I laugh too hard,
At the jokes my friends conceal.

Bling can't hold back the laughter,
When grandma's flower comes undone,
A tug here, a pull there,
Oh, my fashion sense is fun!

So let's parade our mishaps,
With shiny things down the street,
Embellished with laughter's grace,
And a touch of goofy beat.

The Glint of Memory

A shiny thing in my pocket,
From a date I can't recall,
It glints like a lost secret,
Or maybe just a bad fall.

It's shaped like a goofy critter,
A croaking frog or a bear,
I wore it to impress my date,
Now it's lost without a care.

Each time I glance at that bauble,
I chuckle at who I chased,
Memories pinned on fabric,
With giggles graced and misplaced.

So here's for bright reflections,
In this life that's truly wild,
May our sparkly little treasures,
Keep us laughing, love unbiled.

Adornment of Wishes

I found a pin shaped like a star,
To adorn a wish or two,
But it points to the wrong direction,
Now my dreams are set askew.

Each clasp holds a secret hope,
Like wearing my heart on my sleeve,
But when I tried to impress,
The clasp simply wouldn't believe.

They say wishes come true by night,
With sparkle and charm they'll glide,
Yet here I am, tangled up,
In the glitter I cannot hide.

So let's wear our goofy wishes,
Like fanciful hats in a row,
For each charm tells a story,
Of laughter we've come to know.

The Clasp of Connection

I saw a clip in a store,
That promised friendship for life,
But it slipped and fell in the soup,
The start of a delightful strife.

It blinged with the joy of laughter,
Each sparkle a snicker and more,
Who knew connections were slippery,
And that they'd turn into folklore?

Each friend I've pinned to my heart,
With a clasp that could hold a dream,
Turns out they pop off the fabric,
And waddle away, or so it seems.

Let's toast to the bonds that snag,
Over coffee, tea, or a torte,
For even with crazy fashion,
It's the laughter we keep for sport.

The Pinning of Memories

Upon my shirt, you took a stance,
A wink of silver, caught my glance.
With every jig, it jives and sways,
A dance of thoughts from younger days.

It holds my secrets, keeps them dear,
Like stories told with jingles near.
When laughter bubbles, it won't hide,
A gem of joy, my sleepless guide.

Each poke and prod, a tale unfolds,
Of rubber bands and marbles, bold.
In pockets deep, it found a home,
Through ups and downs, where memories roam.

So here's to pins that save the day,
In heart's attire, they come to play.
We stitch our lives with playful glee,
Embellished quirks, just you and me.

A Jewel in the Chest of Feelings

In the chest where treasures lie,
A glimmer caught the corner's eye.
A saucy gem, with stories packed,
Of battles won and snacks exact.

It sparkles bright in morning light,
A privilege of my wardrobe's might.
When asking where my joy may roam,
This shiny piece feels just like home.

Each color tells a different tale,
Of midnight snacks and ships that sail.
With every clasp, a little cheer,
The laughter rings, I hold it near.

Oh, what a gem! It shines so true,
Of silly moments, it knows a few.
With every twirl and fashion flip,
It's laughter that gives my heart a dip.

Heartfelt Accents of Love

Accents on my collar bright,
Who knew they could bring such delight?
With every glance, a silly wink,
It's both a treasure and a link.

Decked in charms, I strut around,
My chest of fun, with joy profound.
Each little clip holds playful schemes,
A laughter's thread weaves through my dreams.

With silly pins as backup crew,
They lift me up like morning dew.
On days when frowns attempt a fight,
These quirky bits restore my light.

Oh, heartfelt accents, shining bright,
In every joke, they join the fight.
So gather round, let's show our flair,
In love's embrace, we're light as air.

The Clasps of Care

Clasps of care on casual wear,
Like hugs that follow me everywhere.
Stitch and twirl, we laugh and play,
These twinkling treasures, come what may.

Each fastening tells its own charm,
With playful nudges, they disarm.
Through ups and downs, come watch us glide,
These silly pins are joy's sweet ride.

With every clasp, a tale we weave,
Of happy hearts, we won't deceive.
In closets full of quirk and jest,
This clumsy love is just the best.

So here's to seals that simply cheer,
With laughter's echo drawing near.
In every hug and tight embrace,
These clasps of care, our warmest place.

The Heart's Hidden Gem

In a lovely box, it sits so tight,
A sparkly thing, oh what a sight!
Stuck to my chest, feels like a joke,
Am I a fashionista, or just a bloke?

Found it at a thrift shop, what a find,
Thought it was a cat, oh never mind!
Twinkling at my heart, a bit of flair,
But wait, is that fluff? I shouldn't wear!

The cat's old hair, now it's brand new,
Placed with love, but do I have a clue?
Bling for the ages, it might be cursed,
Should it glimmer bright, or just disperse?

It jangles and jingles, what a scene,
Wearing it proudly, I strut like a queen!
Friends all around, they break into cheer,
While I just wonder, is that my cat's peer?

Love's Gentle Adornment

A shiny pin upon my shirt,
Ready to shine, or just to flirt?
It winks at those who wander near,
Dare you touch? Better steer clear!

Glimmers in the sun, quite the tease,
Hold your pants, where's the breeze?
Poking passion from my chest,
It's humor here, and I love it best!

Each quirky shape tells a tale,
From Paris to a local sale!
Tangled in tales of love and glee,
Is it art, or just kitchery?

When I wear it, laughter takes flight,
Fancies aglow, oh what a sight!
A love so goofy, why not embrace?
Decked in this charm, I'm full of grace!

Radiant Tokens of Devotion

A little pin that's quite absurd,
Adorning me like a fluffy bird!
Brooches together, what a parade,
On days I can't find my charm cascade!

Friends all giggle and pinedeck me,
Am I a clown? What do you see?
With each glimmer, there's joy to be found,
Fashion's a laugh, it's all so profound!

Hopping along, it's a dazzling sight,
Fashion faux pas? I wear it with might!
Every little token has a story to share,
In this collection, there's love in the air!

A rainbow of memories snuggled so tight,
Crafted with care, they shine through the night!
Bedecked with glee, in a whimsy embrace,
My heart's a canvas, a wild, funny space!

Keepsakes of the Affectionate

A butterfly pinned where my heart might roam,
Flapping like it's found a new home!
Laughter leaks from this little charm,
It's all in fun, come see my glam!

Each intricacy tells a tale or two,
Love's funny twists, both me and you!
It's bright and colorful, quite the show,
Oh dear, does everyone see my bow?

Crinkly edges and colors that clash,
Is it a brooch or a colorful trash?
Worn with pride, it begs to be known,
An odd little treasure that feels like home!

Friends tease me gently, but I don't mind,
This goofy sparkle is one of a kind!
So here I stand, with flair and quirk,
In this love fest, I'll happily lurk!

An Ornament of Intimacy

A sparkly clip, oh what a sight,
It glimmers bright in morning light.
It holds together bits of flair,
Like mismatched socks or wild hair.

Each day I wear it, quite a show,
It dances lightly, high and low.
Friends giggle near, no secrets kept,
As stories swirl where laughter leapt.

A playful charm, a silly jest,
It shows my heart, I must confess.
With quirky pins and doodled art,
It anchors joy, and that's the start.

So here I am, with flair so grand,
A trinket that we understand.
It celebrates the fun we share,
In every wink, in every glare.

Whispered Elegance

A pin that twirls upon my chest,
Its whispers say, 'I'm here, just rest.'
It catches eyes, igniting grins,
An elegant tale where fun begins.

With twinkling gems like fireflies,
It teases truth beneath the guise.
Each glance a giggle, each touch a jest,
It crowns my heart, a silly fest.

It jigs like jelly, winks, and sways,
In mismatched outfits, bold displays.
An ornament of closeness near,
With laughs that spark, we draw each cheer.

So here I flaunt my playful prize,
With charm that lights up dreary skies.
It sings of fondness, cheeky, bright,
And keeps our secrets wrapped in delight.

Heartstrings Entwined

A quirky piece that makes me beam,
Its charm unravels every dream.
Stuck on with care, it twists and bends,
A badge of humor, joy transcends.

It laughs with me, like a best friend,
Our shared adventures never end.
In wild colors, it tells our tale,
Through winks and nudges, we set sail.

With each small jingle, light and fun,
It teases life, and then we run.
It anchors all our silly plans,
With dance of laughter in its hands.

A fabric woven with threads so tight,
It gleams with mischief, pure delight.
Together we'll skip through laughter's art,
Boldly wearing joy, heart to heart.

Starlit Tokens of Connection

Oh, what a gem upon my chest,
A shining piece that knows the best.
With winks that shimmer like the stars,
It bands my heart, no room for scars.

Each night it twirls in moonlit dance,
A tribute to our silly chance.
Like secret smiles and hidden laughs,
It holds my hopes in playful halves.

The world may be a serious place,
But on my heart, it finds its grace.
With clasp and sparkle, it stays near,
Connecting moments, joy sincere.

So wear your trinkets, have a blast,
With laughter glowing, shadows cast.
These starlit pieces, bold and bright,
Will keep our spirits soaring in flight.

An Heirloom of Emotion

In grandma's drawer, I found a thing,
A shiny piece, like a bizarre ring.
It jiggled and jangled, a curious site,
I swear it winked at me, what a fright!

With odd colors flashing, it seemed to play,
Like a disco party on a boring day.
I pinned it on, feeling quite grand,
Next thing I knew, I was in demand!

A dinner invite, oh the spice of fate,
But no one warned me, the brooch is fate!
It snagged on the table, oh the disgrace,
I bowed and blushed, what a silly place!

So here's to treasures, both wacky and wild,
Holding my heart like a mischievous child.
A memory or two, it certainly stirs,
With a wink and a giggle, oh how it purrs!

The Fastening of Sentiments

I clasp my feelings with a shiny pin,
A little sparkle, where do I begin?
The lock of laughter, oh how it shines,
Like a cat in sunbeams, on playful vines.

Stuck on my chest like a proud display,
It waves at the world in a cheeky way.
Thoughts filtered through laughter, not quite refined,
Just how many quirks can one heart unwind?

Each tap of my heart makes it jiggle about,
As friends lean in close, with a playful shout.
It grabs their attention and keeps them near,
Oh, the stories it tells as we sip our beer!

In a world of sincerity, such humor we weave,
With pins and attachments, it's hard to believe.
So fasten your feelings, let the fun reign,
In a world of metal, love's never mundane!

Pins and Promises

Upon my lapel, a curious bit,
It whispers sweet tales, oh what a hit!
A secret keeper, mishaps and cheer,
Labels me 'charming,' oh dear, oh dear!

Like a shy child, it peeks and it hides,
Being a spoiler when laughter collides.
A tchotchke of joy that tickles the soul,
But darn it gets snagged on my shirt, oh control!

Every party I attend, it takes center stage,
The life of the gathering, acting its age.
It flaps and it flails, in mirth it displays,
This pin of mischief, in merry arrays.

Jokes tangled in threads, oh what a mess,
Promises made, can we love and confess?
In the gallery of laughter, it proudly adorns,
With life in its pins, a family of thorns!

The Brooch Beneath the Skin

A curious thing, not part of my kin,
Yet it feels like family, let's let the fun spin.
Beneath the surface, it chuckles and purrs,
This trinket I wear, my heart in a blur.

It watches my moves, like a lifelong mate,
Poking fun gently, what a grand fate.
With every snicker, it shifts a bit loose,
Oh dear, there it goes! Who thought it would choose?

A dance on my shoulder, what a show it leads,
Each step that I take, it's planting odd seeds.
A promise so silly, though it twinkled bright,
It vows to keep shining throughout the night.

So cherish these moments, this laughter divine,
For pins of affection can cross the line.
With treasures so odd, oh what a delight,
Wear your heart openly, let laughter ignite!

Glimmering Remembrances

In a drawer, it lies so still,
With stories that give me a thrill.
A glittering gem, my past's delight,
It winks at me through endless night.

Grandma wore it in her youth,
It made her dance, uncouth.
Every pin, a tale to tell,
Of loves and laughs, and things that fell.

I fasten it to my coat, you see,
And now I'm dressed with history.
My friends all laugh, they point and tease,
"Where'd you get that? From a flea?"

Yet, every sparkle shines so bright,
It fills my heart, a pure delight.
With every glance, I can't ignore,
These glimmering tales, I crave for more.

A Heart's Talisman

This shiny thing, it holds my heart,
With every brooch, a quirky start.
A talisman that leads my way,
To funny days and memories gay.

In photos, it steals the show,
Turning, twisting, putting on a glow.
My friends just laugh, they shake their heads,
"Your fashion sense is full of dreads!"

It jabs my shirt in wild surprise,
A painful hug that makes me cry.
Yet somehow still, it feels so right,
A heart's pure charm, in morning light.

So I prance out, with style unmatched,
In every glance, I feel attached.
A silly pin, but dear to me,
A heart's sweet treasure, wild and free.

Shadows of the Shimmer

In closets deep, the shadows play,
Where shimmering memories still sway.
Each sparkle hums a silly tune,
Of days that flirt with afternoon.

A phantom pin, with stories vast,
From high school crushes to ages past.
It reminds me of a grand mischief,
When I wore it wrong, and caused a rift.

"Oh dear," I said, "please don't take stock!"
As laughter echoed, I felt a shock.
Little did I know, they'd find me thus,
A joke of fashion, just for us!

Now shadows dance with every twinkle,
A glimmer here and there, a wrinkle.
In every laugh, I feel that grace,
Those shimmering days, my favorite place.

The Pinch of Nostalgia

A pinch of this, a sprinkle that,
My quirky pin looks like a cat!
With whiskers wide, it winks at foes,
And often proves to steal the show.

Nostalgia nips, it makes me gasp,
With tales of laughs and kisses clasped.
At gatherings, it wears a grin,
Inviting chuckles, basking in sin!

"Is that your style?" my friend inquired,
"Your taste was never so inspired!"
Still I wore it, proud and loud,
In its presence, I feel so proud.

So here's to pins that tell a tale,
With giggles shared and few that fail.
A pinch of fun, a dash of heart,
In fashion's game, I've played my part.

Heartfelt Affixations

On my chest, a shiny gem,
A quirky bird, a little stem,
It flaps around, with all its might,
A laugh each day, just feels so right.

This quirky piece, a chatterbox,
It tells my heart all sorts of knocks,
When I forget my coffee cup,
It shouts, 'Hey, don't give up!'.

Each hug can lead to silly sounds,
Dancing around as joy abounds,
It teases all my close-knit friends,
With jokes that never seem to end.

A twist of fate, an evening wear,
A sneaky wink, my gem's aware,
It knows I'd rather joke than cry,
So here we laugh, just you and I.

A Pendant of Memories

With anchors deep in every tale,
A trinket worn, it cannot fail,
It swings and sways, a tiny jest,
A playful heart within my vest.

Each memory shines like a bright star,
A tale of love, from near and far,
It whispers soft when days get grey,
'Take a break, come dance and play!'

A locket filled with silly things,
A jester's cap, oh how it swings,
It makes me chuckle, brings me cheer,
In moments small, it feels so near.

So here I am, with gem in hand,
A charm that lifts like ocean sand,
Through each mishap or foible shared,
We wear our smiles, completely paired.

A Casket of Charm

In my pocket, a treasure lies,
A tiny box with laughing eyes,
It holds my jokes and silly puns,
A joyful heart, oh how it runs!

With every giggle, it will clap,
A playful pulse, a merry tap,
I wear it close when feeling low,
A jester's heart, a spark to show.

Each charm I keep is filled with fun,
A rainbow bright beneath the sun,
It knows the way to lift the gloom,
And turns my frown to joyful bloom.

So gather round, my friends, and see,
This quirky heart is wild and free,
With every beat, it sings of cheer,
In this casket, laughter's near.

The Glow of Emotion

A flicker here, a twinkle there,
This little spark is everywhere,
It dances about, so full of glee,
A giggle fit, come laugh with me!

When life gets tough, it's by my side,
With twinkling eyes, my joy and pride,
It glows like stars when skies are sad,
A silly jest, the best I've had.

It sends a wink into the night,
A bubbled laugh, oh what a sight,
It knows that moments dark might loom,
But humor's light will fill the room.

So let us toast, to joy's bright spark,
To laughter shared, to light the dark,
In every hue, this heart still glows,
With joy that only friendship knows.

Gilded Reminiscences

In a jewelry box, laughter lies,
Sparkling moments under bright skies.
A rusted pin, once bold and bright,
Now just a relic, a comical sight.

Memories jingle like charm bracelets,
Funny tales of previous mistakes.
A dance on the table, a toast from a mug,
Every mishap, a warm, fuzzy hug.

With each twist, a story unfurls,
About that time, oh, how it twirls!
A misplaced clasp, a fashion faux pas,
Yet we strut like stars, a comedy far.

So here's to the flair, the sparkle we wear,
In life's big picture, we all have our share.
Laughter's the gem that never will fade,
In this golden heart, the jokes are well laid.

The Weight of Beauty

A locket heavy with secrets untold,
Bound with the laughter of ages old.
Once it was polished, now it's quite lame,
Yet still it sparkles, playing the game.

Amusingly stuck in a fashion time warp,
The clasp has a jiggle, a jovial larp.
Trendy it isn't, yet loved it remains,
Worn like a crown on the goofball's reign.

Funny how beauty has a strange heft,
Tales of the past, give laughter bereft.
Its charms are all twisted, yet quirky and bright,
In the heart of the jest, it feels just right.

So laugh at the weight of what we hold dear,
With every odd thing, comes joy and some cheer.
For beauty's a giggle, just hang it on tight,
In the shop of the heart, it shines through the night.

A Seal on the Heart

A quirky stamp with a heart so bold,
Comical moments in stories retold.
Sealed with a giggle, adorned with a sigh,
Each time we stumble, it's all worth a try.

Fridge magnets twirl, snapshots don't align,
A heart's silly stamp, oh what a design!
Imperfectly perfect, it dances and sings,
Chasing our worries, it's just silly things.

Every embrace is a quirk in disguise,
With playful winks and mischievous eyes.
A seal made of laughter, a chuckle or two,
Binding together a jovial crew.

So treasure the laughter, let it have its say,
In the book of affection, it lights up the gray.
For love's not just serious, it's playful and sweet,
With a seal on our hearts, it's a funny retreat.

Accents of Affection

A quirky pin with a rainbow bright,
Accents of laughter, all wrapped up tight.
Pinched on the collar, a gumdrop of cheer,
Woven with giggles, it draws you near.

With doodles of love all scribbled in gold,
Every little quirk, a delight to behold.
Sparkling nonsense, a whimsical flair,
Love is a fashion with room to spare.

A wobbly gemstone, a crooked charm,
Each twist makes you laugh, it's got its own charm.
In a world full of fuss, let humor ignite,
For accents of fondness can keep you alight.

So wear all your laughter like glittering art,
Dress your affection in shadows and spark.
In this playful parade of love's sweet embrace,
Accents of affection make life a parade.

A Touch of Sentiment

In a box of laughter, feelings stored,
A shiny trinket that I adored.
It jabs my chest like a quick little bee,
Where humor and warmth dance happily.

With glittering layers and a wink so bright,
It tickles my heart with sheer delight.
An odd little charm, both fancy and fun,
A smile on my shirt, where mischief is spun.

It jangles and jingles, such joyous sounds,
As I prance through life, it twirls all around.
Every giggle I share, it joins the parade,
A cheeky companion, never afraid.

Wrapped in my sentiment, it's quite a sight,
A curious piece of love so light.
This gleeful adornment, perched with glee,
Makes silly memories that cling onto me.

Ornamented Emotions

A shiny pin with a silly toast,
It holds all my secrets, though laughter's the most.
A heart on my sleeve, that wink in the eye,
Gives joy to the serious, as time flits by.

With a twirl of sequins, it flashes and spins,
Whispering tales of my whimsical wins.
This little bauble has seen me trip,
While laughing at life, I can't help but skip.

At brunch, it reminds me, 'Keep spirits light!'
It wobbles and jiggles, a true delight.
A laugh or two, it sparks in a blur,
With this spirited gem, let happiness stir.

Clipped on my shirt, oh goofiness reigns,
Awash in humor, it loosens the chains.
An ornament bold, with a glint of the funny,
These emotions it brings, all sweet and sunny.

The Lattice of Love

In a web of giggles, we stitch our delights,
With fondness and folly that sparkles so bright.
A pun here, a joke there, it's laughter entwined,
This lattice of love is whimsically designed.

It's a tangle of threads, each laugh like a knot,
Each silly remark, a gift that I've got.
With whimsy at play, and awkward embrace,
Our friendship's a collage, a true saving grace.

Beneath the surface, where chuckles reside,
This quilt of emotions, let humor abide.
A pinch of each story, together they weave,
A tapestry fine, where we both believe.

So here's to the lattice, both funky and true,
In each playful poke, we find something new.
With love as our thread, we'll dance through the cheer,
In this comical realm, forever we'll steer.

Intricate Keepsakes

Each piece is a memory, a jibe and a jest,
Intricately crafted, they shine with the best.
This quirky collection, a treasure, not trash,
Makes folly and friendship an iconic splash.

From ribbons to buttons, a playful array,
They hang on my neck, they brighten my day.
A quirky assemblage, each tells a tale,
With laughter and whimsy, our hearts will not fail.

In pockets and pouches, we store our delight,
Keepsakes of folly, that sparkle so bright.
Through giggles and snorts, each glorious piece,
Brings smiles that reflect life's playful release.

As I flip through my treasures, on this merry ride,
With laughter's embrace, I take all in stride.
Each intricate charm pulls my heart in a dance,
In this joyful collection, we'll take a chance.

The Glint of Togetherness

When laughter clinks like polished gold,
We wear our joys, bright and bold.
Each joke a gem caught in the light,
Our smiles shine through day and night.

In pockets deep, we hide small charms,
Like little tricks with quirky arms.
They dangle, they dance, making us grin,
A treasure trove of fun within.

Oh, how we twinkle with mischief's spark,
Like fireflies that light up the park.
In every jest, our hearts do play,
Together, we'll glow in a silly way.

So here's to bonds with laughter sewn,
In every quirk, our love is shown.
We glint like stars, a vibrant team,
With humor stitched in every seam.

Woven Threads of Affection

Life's a tapestry of goofy threads,
With silly patterns that dance in our heads.
Each laugh a stitch, each pun a tie,
We weave our joy as days whisk by.

In corners bright, our colors spin,
Like mismatched socks, we're both all in.
With every quip, we knot our fate,
Creating joy that's first-rate great.

Together we twirl, just like a reel,
In this fabric of love, we make it real.
Our quirks are buttons, a playful stash,
With every moment, we create a splash.

So here's to threads of laughter's glow,
In this fabric of life, may our joy overflow.
With every stitch, we create our art,
In the woven quilt of each goofy heart.

Whispers of Adornment

In the silly shadows of a party tight,
We wear our smiles, oh such a sight.
With whispers soft, we crack our jokes,
Like shiny badges on friendly folks.

Each laugh we wear, a tiny prize,
With sparkle that twinkles in our eyes.
Our hearts adorned with fun and cheer,
Like comic book heroes, we hold dear.

Oh, how we giggle, twirled around,
In this playful dance, we are unbound.
With every quirk, we strut with flair,
Our joy is a gem that floats in the air.

So let's adorn our journey bright,
With laughter's jewels, a true delight.
In every joke, our hearts ignite,
In whispers sweet, we feel so light.

Emblems of Affection

Like shiny badges, we wear our glee,
With every giggle, just you and me.
Our quirks like buttons on a coat,
In this playful swirl, we take a float.

Each pun we share, a badge of pride,
In laughter's lap, we take a ride.
With every jest, our bond does spark,
We light up life, oh what a lark.

So here's to icons of our delight,
With silly symbols shining bright.
In every chuckle, a moment's art,
Our friendship glows, a joyful heart.

Let's wear our joy like crowns so grand,
In the kingdom of laughter, hand in hand.
With our emblems bold, we'll spread the cheer,
Creating memories we hold dear.

Insignia of the Unseen

A pin that holds my joy so tight,
In the morning glare, it steals the sight.
It dances on my chest with glee,
Mocking me, oh so easily!

Caught in fabric, what a sight,
I chase it down, oh what a fight!
With every hug, it tries to flee,
A runaway badge, just like me!

I wear my heart, in shiny bliss,
But every hug's a peekaboo kiss.
This tiny charm, my daily jest,
Clinging on, it knows me best!

So here's to pins and playful laughs,
In every mishap, joy just halves.
A badge of humor on my chest,
Making life's moments feel the best!

The Art of Attachment

In my wardrobe, it sits so proud,
This tiny jewel, like a laughing crowd.
It waves goodbye when I lean to kiss,
Holding on tight, can't let it miss!

With every outfit, it comes to play,
Turning grey mornings bright and gay.
Lost in the shuffle, it giggles loud,
My fashion friend, a quirky cloud!

When dinner's served, it goes for a ride,
Skewered by dinner rolls, it can't hide.
A culinary journey, oh what a flair,
Just hope the gravy won't call for a prayer!

Behind every clasp, a story awaits,
Each twist and turn, it celebrates.
In laughter and mischief, it won't part,
For wearing joy is an art from the heart!

Captured in Metal

This shiny pin, oh what a tease,
Tangles my ties with utmost ease.
Like a pet cat, it's hard to control,
Pouncing and jumping, oh what a goal!

It sticks around when I start to dance,
My partner in mischief, given the chance.
With every twirl, it gives a shout,
A medal for chaos, no doubt about!

Sometimes it slips and gives a fright,
Jumps off my chest in the dead of night.
Searching the floor like a madcap chase,
Who knew a pin could win such a race?

Silver and gold, my trusty friend,
With laughter and giggles, it never ends.
In the scrapbook of life, it plays its part,
Captured in metal, and close to my heart!

Preserved in Today

Behold my pin, a quirky artifact,
It knows my secrets, and that's a fact.
Stuck on my shirt, it can't help but grin,
Does it have feelings? Let the fun begin!

It whispers tales of the times we've had,
From calm to chaos, never a fad.
When I reach for snacks, it takes a chance,
Bobbing and weaving, a daring dance!

This little gem, a time machine,
Tales of mishaps, unlikely and keen.
Like a historian, it gleefully sways,
Preserving my moments in funny ways!

So raise your glass to this shiny friend,
With every laugh, our troubles suspend.
In the book of today, it's quite the start,
For humor and joy go hand in heart!

The Accidental Heirloom

Once found a trinket, bright and round,
On grandma's couch, just lying 'round.
She swore it gleamed with love and care,
But it was just a button, I swear!

I wore it proudly, thinking I'd shine,
Till friends all laughed, said, "That's not divine!"
A button on a string, how could it be?
An heirloom? Just a joke, it seems to me!

Next, I found a pin, shaped like a cat,
Who knew such things could cause such chat?
I wore it boldly to a fancy feast,
Proving heirlooms could be quite the beast!

Confused looks followed every step I took,
Praise for the style they simply mistook.
What's old is new, or so I liked to claim,
Yet laughter took the charm, and I took the blame!

Glimpses of treasure are everywhere,
Hidden in pockets, if you dare!
Found a comb that sparkled in the light,
Forgotten from a dance—oh, what a sight!

So here's to relics that make us smile,
Though mysterious, they're worth all the while.
In laughter and joy, let memories flow,
For in silly trinkets, true love can grow!

Heartbound Adornments

A pendant shaped like a slice of pie,
I wore it proudly, oh my, oh my!
Friends asked if it symbolized my snack,
I said, "No way! It's love, and that's a fact!"

Each charm a blunder, each clasp a joke,
Who knew that accessories could provoke?
A tie that jingled with every move,
What heart can resist in this crazy groove?

Found a bracelet, half a dozen beads,
Claiming it tied together all my needs.
But it broke at dinner, oh what a mess,
Like my secrets spilling, no more finesse!

Next, a ring I swore brought luck my way,
Until I lost it on a rainy day.
The moral is clear, don't wear with flair,
You might just become the grinning bear!

Oh, jewelry that makes no sense at all,
Funky, mixed-match, like a kid's play ball.
Let's wear our stories, laugh till we cry,
In heartbound adornments, we aim for the sky!

Emblem of Unspoken Bonds

A locket lost with pictures of snacks,
Who needs love when there's chips in stacks?
Each friend just chuckles when they take a peek,
"Your heart's full of flavors - what a unique streak!"

Next, I found a charm shaped like a shoe,
That says, "Run fast from drama, it's true!"
I wore it to work, raised my eyebrows high,
Who knew such humor made spirits fly?

An eraser pendant that's poorly made,
Represents all the mistakes I've laid.
"You can wipe them away, so have no fear,"
Laughter erupted—my motto was clear!

Two spoons linked together, what could they mean?
"Let's dish out the stories that haven't been seen!"
They jiggled and jangled with every small laugh,
An emblem of bonds that cut trouble in half!

Hold tight to the pieces that seem out of place,
For laughter and love's our saving grace.
Each clink and each clatter lays bare some delight,
In silly adornments, our hearts take flight!

Heartfelt Charms

A rubber ducky, all shiny and bright,
Hanging from my neck—oh, what a sight!
"Quackers for love," my friends teased, so bold,
But who knew a charm could break the mold?

A necklace made up of tiny cheese wheels,
Proving my passion for oddball feels.
They ask, "Is that cheddar or gouda?" I grin,
"Just serving up joy from the place I've been!"

Oh, buttons and clips, each color absurd,
Fashion statements that spoke without word.
People just chuckle, some even stare,
Who knew such silly could light up the air?

With charms of all kinds, let's give it a whirl,
Throw on the oddities — give 'em a twirl!
For heartfelt adornments are meant to shout,
That laughter and love are what this life's about!

So here's to the quirks, from pets to delight,
Worn with a grin, joyful and light.
In laughter we find our connections so sweet,
With heartfelt charms, our hearts skip a beat!

The Heart's Secret Charm

In the chest lies a treasure, oh what a delight,
Swaying and jingling, it dances at night.
A tiny pin whispers secrets untold,
Wearing its magic, oh, quite bold!

Laughter erupts when it twirls around,
With every step, new joy can be found.
It tickles the ribs, it pokes fun at despair,
Like an impish sprite, it's always aware.

It sits with a flair, so proud on my chest,
Surveying the world, giving life its best.
Who knew such a trinket could spark so much mirth?
A playful twist on this wild, wacky earth!

So, here's to the moments of giggles and glee,
Where this cheeky little gem dances like a bee.
With a wink and a smile, it brings forth the cheer,
Keeping the heart light, year after year.

Emotional Embellishments

Grinning like a fool on my shirt it resides,
With flair and with style, it has nothing to hide.
A vivid reminder of whimsical dreams,
It giggles and chortles, or so it seems.

When life gives a frown, just give it a twist,
This pin's got the power, you can't resist.
It's a wink from the cosmos, a chuckle divine,
Like a sparkly shout, 'Hey, life can be fine!'

In the pocket of joy, it jingles with cheer,
Woven with laughter, a friendship sincere.
Through all of our trials, it brings such a lift,
A glittering token, a charming gift.

So gather your laughter and wear it like pride,
Let the pin sprinkle joy, all day as your guide.
In emotional flair, may it never depart,
A charming reminder, straight from the heart!

Poised Beneath the Skin

Sassy and sneaky, a gem tucked away,
It winks from my neckline throughout the day.
With mischief in mind, it playfully gleams,
Spreading pure joy like the sun's golden beams.

A pocket of giggles, oh, it knows the score,
This feisty accessory delights to explore.
Ready for banter, it thrives on the jest,
A crafty companion, it thinks of the best!

When life takes a dip and tries to offend,
It tickles the soul and insists it won't end.
With charm so alive, it combats the gloom,
A shining example of joy in full bloom.

So let it adorn you with laughter and cheer,
Poised just beneath, spreading joy far and near.
In the dance of the funny, together we play,
This playful little gem lights up the way!

Jewel of Kindred Spirits

Sparkling and bright, a connector so fine,
This emblem of joy makes everything shine.
With a giggle and wink, it opens the gate,
To friendships that flourish, never too late.

It tells silly stories, sweet moments, and laughs,
A whimsical charm that loves all the paths.
Strutting its stuff with a bold little bounce,
Provoking chuckles, an endless renounce.

Emotional kinship, it twirls in delight,
Linking heart to heart, a spectacular sight.
In gatherings of laughter, it's always the star,
A jewel for the ages, no matter how far.

So cherish this trinket, a symbol so bright,
Sprinkling humor like starlight at night.
For the bonds of our spirits it endlessly weaves,
A funny little treasure that the heart believes.

www.ingramcontent.com/pod-product-compliance
Lightning Source LLC
Chambersburg PA
CBHW060113230426
43661CB00003B/169